Love, Devotion, Surrender

...and other bright ideas

Poetry and Lyrics
from the early 21ST Century and beyond
by
MARTIN FAWKES

---

oceandeep
PRESS

All works © Martin Fawkes

Cry, Fall Out, Half My Knowledge, Seconds, Wound, You Paying? © 1999

Don't Need, Far, Grace (Spirit), I Want To Put A Name To It, Speak Soft, Unfog © 2000

Fathom, Last © 2001

Best I Ever, Every Little Bit Counts. Sometimes, Here, Love Remains, Shine © 2002

Obscurer © 2003

Come With Me, The Girl Who Died of Option Frenzy, Icarus: Dream Of Flight, Icarus: Ascent, Icarus Descending: Pact Impact, Icarus: Transcend, Paraglyph; Paraclete, Psychologie: Analysis, Prognosis © 2004

After Rainfall, Arbitrary, Dereliction, Envision, Escapeness, Etcetera & C., Parachuted, Praise, Redeem, Ste Go © 2005

Castle Keep © 2007

Notice © 2008

Awaken, Good, Taste, A World to Change © 2009

An Ordinary Walk/A More Interesting Walk, Mining, Required © 2010

Annoy, Arrowing, Chivalry, Nauticaa (Ocean Breathe), Noise Factor, Not So Worse, Paranoia Takes Two, Silence, The Subtle Ties, To Change a World, Your Voice © 2011

A Day Late But Right On Time, Beginning The World, Lose Hold, Nonplus, Simplify, Takes Nothing, Vise, You Win © 2012

Departure, Even If Ever © 2013

All Shook Down, Fade Out, Groundless, Imperceptible, Makeshift, Point Out the Stars, Speechless, The W Rises © 2024

Anything, Cold Fire, Masque © 2025

Cover image by Lucian Coman www.luciancoman.com licensed from istockphoto.com

Interior artwork adapted from "St. Albans Starlight"

by Chris Fawkes © www.chrisfawkes.com

LOVE
DEVOTION
SURRENDER
...and other bright ideas

ISBN 978-0-6456419-1-2

Published by

OCEANDEEP

PO Box 4264

Geelong VIC 3220 Australia

www.oceandeep.au

> "Life is what happens to you
> while you're busy
> making other plans"
> John Lennon

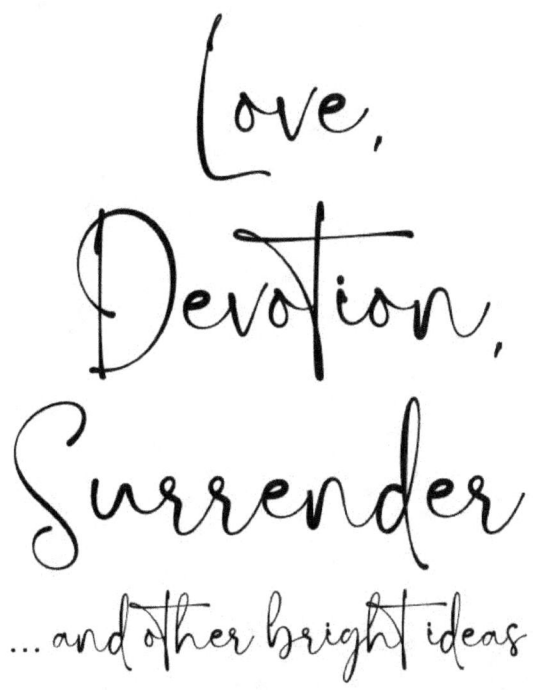

Poetry and Lyrics
from the early 21ST Century and beyond
by
MARTIN FAWKES

oceandeep
PRESS

CONTENTS

PART ONE: LOVE AND AFFECTION

An Ordinary Walk ✳ A More Interesting Walk ✳ After Rainfall ✳ All Shook Down ✳ Anything ✳ Annoy ✳ Arbitrary ✳ Arrowing ✳ Beginning the World ✳ Best I Ever ✳ Castle Keep ✳ Chivalry ✳ Cold Fire ✳ Come With Me ✳ Cry

PART TWO: DEVOTION AND DIRECTION

A Day Late But Right On Time ✳ Departure ✳ Dereliction ✳ Don't Need ✳ Envision ✳ Escapeness ✳ Etcetera & C. ✳ Even If Ever ✳ Every Little Bit Counts. Sometimes. ✳ Fade Out ✳ Fall Out ✳ Far ✳ Fathom ✳ The Girl Who Died of Option Frenzy ✳ Good ✳ Grace (Spirit) ✳ Groundless ✳ Half My Knowledge ✳ Here ✳ I Want To Put a Name To It ✳ Imperceptible

PART THREE: SURRENDER AND INSURRECTION

Icarus: Dream of Flight ✳ Icarus: Ascent ✳ Icarus Descending: Pact Impact ✳ Icarus: Transcend ✳ Last ✳ Lose Hold ✳ Love Remains ✳ Makeshift ✳ Masque ✳ Mining ✳ Nauticaa (Ocean Breathe) ✳ Noise Factor ✳ Not So Worse ✳ Notice ✳ Obscurer ✳ Parachuted ✳ Paraglyph; Paraclete ✳ Paranoia Takes Two ✳ Point Out the Stars ✳ Praise ✳ Psychologie: Analysis, Prognosis ✳ Redeem

PART FOUR: EVERYTHING ELSE UNDER THE SUN

Required ✳ Seconds ✳ Shine ✳ Silence ✳ Simplify ✳ Speak Soft ✳ Speechless ✳ Stop Go ✳ The Subtle Ties ✳ Takes Nothing ✳ Taste ✳ To Change a World ✳ Unfog ✳ Vise ✳ The Wind Rises ✳ A World to Change ✳ Wound ✳ You Paying? ✳ You Win ✳ Your Voice

AN INTRODUCTION:

The Greek philosopher Heraclitus once infamously said no-one ever steps in the same river twice, as it is not the same river and they are not the same person.

But is it the river that's changed, or just the water?

And who was I when I wrote so many of the pieces in this collection?

Someone younger, for sure. The same me, but different. But the same, but me.

You'll find in these pages poetry from some of the chapbooks I put together several years ago, *Songs and Silent Prayers*, *Word Jazz* and *A Book of Fridays*, some of it slightly reworked; plus a handful of never before published newer pieces.

Putting *Love Devotion, Surrender* together has been an intriguing chance to revisit more youthful me and my earlier writings downstream.

A revisit of the old poetic river, mostly the same but sometimes subtly different.

And so, welcome to
Love, Devotion Surrender and other bright ideas.

Dive deep!

Love and Affection

1: AN ORDINARY WALK

I went for a walk
I took my phone
With me to talk
To my nearest and dearest
(But sometimes a-fearest)
Nowhere near the forest
Neither Nor-East nor Nor-West
I wanted to go for a stroll
Nice day for it
P'raps a bit cold
No rain in the sky
It's all in my eye
And I need the exercise
(So I'm told).

2. A MORE INTERESTING WALK

I feel it in my knees
Every footfall, but somehow
I need to see
What's at the end of my intention
Just a little walk
A bit of exercise
Some subtle, physical
Reinvention of me

AFTER RAINFALL

Pack away your umbrella girl
Let the sweetness of the rain collide
So gently in your hair, against your skin
Breathe and take it in
And let it rain
Let it cleanse and wash away your heartache
Let it rain

Heart of my heart
What ails or redeems ya?
What renews ya right now?
Not close but not so far

Terra firma ground beneath your feet
Hold fast to the gravity
Despite the call to levity
Though the air would taste so sweet

A journey of a thousand miles
Eats lots of little steps
And bloodied though the knees and shins
And wearied as the brow begins
To darken, look ahead
to the horizon that you see
The lights of that city
Right there, shining
Through the trees

ALL SHOOK DOWN

Did you find
What you were looking for?
Did you break
Down
What was blocking up that door?

Were you gonna wait a minute
Pause, reflect just what was in it
A little
Situation
Waiting at the platform
for that late, last train
to nowhere

All shook, all shook
Out and about
Round and round
All shook down

Start the motor
Begin the day
Ignition on, drop the clutch
You're under way
Did you find, did you find
What you were looking for?
Did you break, break, break
Down
What was locking, blocking up
That door?

ANNOY

Botheration
Indignation
Some things are worth saying
This may not be one of them
Is it worth it
A few words on paper
Melody, harmony
Catch cry or murmur
Disbar the despair
Hum me a few bars
I'll see if I can
Bother playing along
This empty song

ANYTHING

If I could tell you anything
I would surely tell you everything
But we made a little deal
To know only what we know

Nothing more & nothing less
Maybe we gave it all our best
What is best in show?
Did someone pay off all the judges
Leaving me alone
And leaving you alone
Who would do such a thing?
I cannot know

ARBITRARY

Do you need a reason?
Who can say, who can tell
Sometimes any decide at all
Is better than waiting for the day-end bell

Can't be free
While you're waiting for the clocks to chime
Lose yourself in time
Or wander lost and lonely though
Until the day is through
Can't find a point of view to see
It almost aways better
Than it's been

ARROWING

Get to the point she said
I thought oh not again
So many simple words
Right there for the saying
C'mon, c'mon and spit it out

Get to the point
She would have said it
If I was listening
To the voices in her head
But she just raised one eyebrow
A tilting of the chin
Expecting me to know
All the things she's thinking

An arrow to the heart
Makes a point you can't deny
Life as sweet as honey
And the stings of humming hives

Arrow, point that arrow
At my heartline
Keep your focus on the narrow
Little punchline
Fire away, no waiting
For another sign
Hit the target, narrow down your vision
Open up your eyes
Make the clear decision
To see what's here
To see what's here

BEGINNING THE WORLD

I am trying
I am trying
For the shout of recognition
Crank up the ignition

I am trying
I am trying
Start the car
Won't get too far
Without your cheer
Without you here

The world is coming to a place of ending
I better hurry
There's a letter waiting
To be written
My little world collapse-accord
begin it all again
The story gets rewritten
Once shy now twice bitten
Begin and taste it all

I am trying
I am trying
To push the plow uphill
How right can I get grooving
Churn the earth
And get things moving here

I am trying
I am trying
To wake the long-time sleepers
Find the lostness and be keeping
All the secret things
No one thought worth anything
But you are here now
You are here now

The world is coming to a place begin again
I hurry there's a story waiting
All written in my brain
Now we all begin again
It all begins again
Trying to begin
It all begins again
Trying to begin it all
Trying to begin it all
Trying to begin it all
Begins
Begins again

BEST I EVER

I think you're the best I ever saw
I think you are so wonderful
I think you're the end of all my dreaming
I think you're the start of all I need

But what do I know?
Why do I think I qualify
To begin to work you out?
To have any kind of claim
On who you really are
Or might be

You're just the best I ever
Just the best I ever
Just the best I ever saw

You confound me and confuse me
You amaze me and amuse me
You surprise me every time I look at you
You are stardust, you are golden
You are what you are, 'yourself'
Don't let me get away with murder
Or anything second best

These are only things I think
How could I know?
Only my opinion
Don't know what could that be worth

You're just the best I ever
Just the best I ever
Just the best I ever saw
Just the best I ever knew

CASTLE KEEP

I hid this battered heart
Inside a wooden box
Wrapped and bound so tight
And hidden out of sight
I hid the box inside a steel bound safe
And put the safe behind
Some thick stone walls
A castle keep
Defended with cannons, spears
Boiling oil and swords

Somehow I build the barricades
Deny you room
Deny you access
But it seems
No power on earth can keep you out
For all I bury, ban or burn
Still you hold my heart

CHIVALRY

If I bought you flowers every day
Could it make the lonely feelings go away?
I'm trying
I'm trying
If I wrote a brand new song for you
Would your heart sing it too?
I'm trying
I'm trying
To be the man for you

If I held each door that kept you out
If I broke the walls of inside out
If I lifted every ceiling
On which you nearly bumped your head
Would it be enough
To keep you cool instead of seeing red?
I'm trying
Working it out
I'm trying
To be the man for you

If I slaughtered every dragon tried to chain your soul
Would it be enough right there
To make your spirit whole?
I put my armour down
Surrender my tarnished crown
Give it all to stop your crying
I'm trying to be the man for you
If it's all that I can do
But not enough
I've been trying, trying
To be the man for you
To be the man for you

COLD FIRE

It's not that I'm not
running around, setting
the world on fire
It just seems like
this old world
don't wanna burn

Not the way I've wanted it to anyway

COME WITH ME ^(COME)

It's over now
So over we could taste it
It's complete somehow
Never needed wasteful moments
No more waiting room
Finite and jejune
Ever after is beckoning
Will you come with me?

We have finished it, the waiting
Moved beyond anticipating
Now for all the evermore
After surviving, striving, reviving
Beyond beginning
Ever after beckons
Whaddya reckon?
Will you come with me?

COME WITH ME ^(STAY)

When weariness is over
Renew at last exhausted limbs
When overcast is overcome
And all dead feeling has gone numb

If time had never called us to this
Why would we then have laboured
And waited for the moment
And waited for the bliss

Faith is done, the hoped for has begun
We see at last, reality
The substance of all we hoped for
Evidence of all we had not seen

Don't settle for the second best
When the hours could be ours
Don't stay portside when all the oceans await

COME WITH ME ^(GO)

Days have passed into history
Between you and I
The artefacts of memory remain
For every precious moment
Hidden or displayed
There is nothing left for sorrow to consume
All that's left is now
All remaining is just us
Let's go, wherever go will be
Come on, now
Come on, come with me

COME WITH ME ^(BE)

Don't despair any longer
You don't have to wait
For the future to begin
All tomorrow seen from yesterday
Begins right now
Let go of all your fear
You're here now
Come with me

CRY

Didn't mean to make you cry
Did I
Did I make you cry?
Just couldn't figure out the contrast
Between the meagre change in my pockets
And what it would cost to make you mine
Can you give it time?

Didn't mean to make you cry
Didn't mean to turn away
Did not intend to be somewhere else
When you finally came my way

The thought had crossed my mind
Maybe you had shed a tear or twelve
Heart wrung out like a bell
Like a moist filled towel twisted and turned
Gripped and ripped, hung then out for air

Didn't mean to make you cry
Didn't mean to let you down
Didn't think to see your gentle smirk come upside down
Didn't mean to make you shine
Didn't mean to lose your smile
Didn't mean to never see you for a while

Didn't mean to make you cry
Didn't mean to turn away
Did not intend to be somewhere other than here
When you finally came my way
When you finally came my way I was away
Don't leave, please don't leave
Don't cry

Devotion and Direction

A DAY LATE BUT RIGHT ON TIME

Tuesday again you made me wait
I'll see your bid and make me mad
With happiness
A day too late but right on time

Thursday fine another time
I felt your breath right down my neck, what the heck
Someone left the door open again, imagine that
A few days late, one time
You will be right on time

You're another day late, another day late
But somehow you're right on time
I was waiting right here anyway
You're another day late, another day late
But somehow you're right on time
I was waiting right here anyway
Any day you're here
Is a good day

Saturday begin again
All the working for the freedom
We could spend it all together
It's the right time
You're another day late, another day late
But somehow you're right on time
I was waiting right here anyway
You're another day late, another day late
But somehow you're right on time
I was waiting right here anyway
Any day you're here
Is a good day

Every moment of anticipation
Is everything for our relating
You make it all worthwhile
You make it all worthwhile
Each moment of anticipation
Builds a brick in our elation
C'mon, smile
Set your watch again
Reset your watch again
And smile for me

You're another day late, another day late
But somehow you're right on time
I was waiting right here anyway
You're another day late, another day late
But somehow you're right on time
I was waiting right here anyway
Any time you're here
Is right on time
I was waiting
Waiting here
Any time you're here
Is right on time

DEPARTURE

All these schemes and plans
Known before the world began
In search of what was dust but dust
Before the holy breath
Now we launch for planet earth
And search for life before death
Not exactly planning an alien invasion
More like a scheme for restoration
Reintroduction of right-relation
Begin agains and born-a-second-time
To deal with entropy, decay and all the rest
The water is alive, so drink it up
And turn to life
Think about it all you need
Then don't think twice

Didn't get there in a rocket ship
Such transport all the way
from there to here
Required a faithful woman's heart and hips

All the comforts of home
Are not quite right
If you're not here

Not an invasion of the alien
But a reversion back to first things
A change of the equation
Back to earth
Back to our favour
All the things of heaven
Ours to savour
Promised in a single birth

DERELICTION

Adriftness isn't all it's cracked up to be
Juiced in all the ocean's finery
Destitute, hirsute and all of fatigue
Hypnoticked by the salty blankets cold and hungry levity
But I remain and do not abandon the slender raft of my hopes
Do your worst, stormy girl
But I wish you'd do your best instead

DON'T NEED

I want you but really I don't believe I need you
So sorry girl, so sorry
My life is full and you would make it so much fun
That I admit
But for all it is and all it's worth
I don't need you to be happy, sorry
Don't need you to be mine

For all those times you held me at arm's length
With twisted lines around my wrists
Connected deep within your heart
You would not let them go
For all those times you held my eyes
And laughter split your lips
You captivate my heart
You hypnotise my soul

But for all it was and all it is
And all these things are worth
I'm so sorry if I let you down by saying this
I want you
But I don't need you to be happy
Don't need you all that close to me
So stay away if that's the game you want to play
Don't need you
I don't need you to be happy

ENVISION

To look at you just one more time
To see behind those eyes
To travel where no human road can take us
To disassemble in ways that human hands can't break us
Reappear renewed reconstituted
Reconstructed in ways that go beyond the blueprints
My giddy heart stops spinning for a moment
And just looks at you...

ESCAPENESS

Straitjacket swims you through the tide
Hugs you like some unwelcome and unwanted bride
Some symbol of another's disdain
Objectify this heart
Wrap it up in buckled cotton
Strap it down in an embrace
Not quite chains but a little of the same

To get free from what holds down your hands
To see and love and live again
It's only this that life demands
How can you be
This free?

ETCETERA & C.

So what comes next
In this grand conversation?
We've said so many things
And now it's been so long

What comes next?
Are words evaporating
Before they're thought
Before they're said
Before they're heard?

I'm just waiting for etcetera &c.
Waiting for beyond the meaningful pause
Waiting for the what-comes-after
Happiness and ever after
Etcetera & c.

EVEN IF EVER

And even if the sky should fall
So sudden block my ears with thunder
Still my heart would hear that call
No wounds to keep you from the wonder

Even if the cage will spill
And leave adrift with sodden seas
No flower fails without departure
Nor eager dreamer flying free

If ever I had lain uncertain
Waiting with uncertain tides
To be aware of every burden
Lost inside the azure skies

Ahold the anchoring decision
For the mention of the fold
Ahead of acclaim and derision
Story spoken and untold

Even if ever I was to tell you
All the telling there is to tell
If ever even I could show you
All of knowing, all be well

Ever even if I knew to
Know you true and know you well
Even if ever I could do so
So I would, all would be well

EVERY LITTLE BIT COUNTS. SOMETIMES.

A bottle of rain on a forest fire
Will not make mud
A grain of sand in river deep
Will not bring flood
A butterfly will beat its wings
Tsunami in Japan?
I don't understand

Every piece you place inside the puzzle
Makes the picture clearer
(Could make the picture clearer)
Every little fractured glimpse
Could clarify it nearer
The little bit can count for so much
Sometimes

A little Wagner just inflames the savage beast
A little mercy bell keeps all those wrists intact
A little silence helps you better say your piece
A little heat can soothe a future full of uncertainties
But where does this all fit?
And what does it all mean?

FADE OUT

Somehow less light
On the situation
Even with the Kliegs
Installed and operating
Dazzle me one or twice
I'm running blind again

FALL OUT

Cast a giant shadow
When the light is angling low
Cast a net over emotion
Spanish seas and look-through-me's
We hesitated before we jumped right in
And found the tide was out
And scraped our shins upon the drying sand
Don't know if I will fall for that one quite agian
But still and all
It was worth the fun of the fall

Raise a giant expectation
What is it you're asking
Climb upon my back to reach the stars
I think I heard my bones begin to crack
Would not begrudge the drudge but who
Will redeem me from this hospital
Don't know, etcetera, and on
Still and all
It was worth the fun of the fall

FAR

Way
Away
Don't, don't, away from me
Sorry words can never heal
The absence of your heart from here

Say
Oh say
But be as well as meaning a place for here
Worry hard can never help you
Stay, not elsewhere be

Come and sip a morning dew
from my lips right here
Come and drink a deeper draught
from the village well
Come and swim an ocean in my eyes
if you can see that far
Will you sink or swim
Or simply flush it all away?

Way
Way
Weigh it all up on the sorrow scales
Balance this with what you've come to know
Stay
Just stay
Or go

FATHOM

"I like you boy" she whispered in my ear
I turned to see my lovely vision disappear
Oh fathom
Oh fathom

It's time she said I saw it written in her eyes
But then she walked away imagine my surprise
Oh fathom
Oh fathom

Fathom, fathom, who can fathom
Fathom, fathom, who can fathom
The heart of a girl
The heart of a girl

If I did not play my cards so closely to my hollow chest
Maybe indecision would not define this mess
If I could only say it loud
If I could only spit it out
If I could only say the words
Maybe my feelings would be heard
If she knew just what I mean
Because my words have made it clear
Maybe she would remain
Perhaps she would be here

Fathom, fathom, who can fathom
Fathom, fathom, who can fathom
The heart of this man
The heart of this man

THE GIRL WHO DIED OF OPTION FRENZY

You drive me sane
You make me sensible
Your ways are plain
You're so dependable

But sadly baby none of this is so
You are the most exciting girl I know

Perhaps profane
Or reprehensible
Full of disdain
So indefensible

Somehow lady none of this is so
You're just the most exciting girl I know

You're so contained
So comprehensible
You are restrained
All ways defensible

Somehow not so much of this is not so so
I'd love to fight it out with all I know
It's all in all an all or nothing show
I'd give you everything
I would spill all of the beans
I'd let you in on all the unsaid things
Before you go
If you'd not go

GOOD

If all I wanted was a moment of your time
Would you mind?
I wonder, would you have minded?

But a little more attention please
If you are so inclined?
Not so kind
Not known to be declining

If this is goodbye
There's nothing good and nothing owned
It's just gone, it's all gone
If this is goodbye
I wish it could be good to say
No more left to pay
No more debt and not more longing for
What is no more

All I want to say
To you today
Three simple words
"Please Go Away"
Until the day
You can say
You got it all out of your system
I will be waiting
I'll still be waiting

I never was so far away
That you weren't on my mind
Is it okay to say hello
To you one more time
How did it feel to know
That you were on my mind?

GRACE (SPIRIT)

Your velvet voice lingers sweetly here
Such words of comfort spoken in my ear
Your kindness unlocking tight wound dreams
Held close these many years
Unwind me free
Unwind me free

Your gentle touch unknots the ache inside my soul
You press, caress and soften
Tense filled feelings
Frozen in the cold
Such singing gentle softening the heart of stone
My chest can hardly hold
Unlock me free
Unlock me free

So salve my wounded body
Wounded spirit
Wounded pride
Arrest my grip
Unlock my hands
To put old clothes aside
Absolve me of my sin
And cleanse my way
And let me see you magnified
Unset me free
Unset me free

GROUNDLESS

Lift off
Take a load off
Step out and catch some air
Come, catch some air
Come, catch some air

Relax, be calm
Unwind, unwind, unwind

I am a kite
And in the face of gale force wind
I will ascend
I will ascend

As it ever was
So it shall ever be
So ever be so
In the end

I am a kite
And in the face of gale force wind
I will ascend
I will ascend

A kite in flight
Don't need to fight against the wind
Relax
Untether
Unwind, unwind, unwind
Ascend
I'm off the ground
I am ascending

HALF MY KNOWLEDGE

Took a bite from bad old tree
Words can't say what I did see
Opened up my sight in a not light way
And though I try
Can't give it half away
Even if I wanted to
Oh' how I wanted to

Now my knowledge, now I knew
Took a bite, rather not now though
Stupid smarts, dumb brains
Couldn't give half my knowledge away
If I wanted to
Oh how I wanted to
Oh yeh

HERE

Change is like holidays
Distant lands and hopes
Why you looking far away?
Turn around
Just turn around
I'm here

Seek sweetness where you will
Hunger and thirst to find your fill
All you need and ever will
It's here
Turn around
Right here

Be my calm
Be my harbor in the storm
My oasis in the dryness
Harbour in the tempest

Shelter me
When shelter is all I need

Evening calls your ships
to sail a dream swept sea
Morning calls to harbor
all that dreams could be

I WANT TO PUT A NAME TO IT

Been searching for a name
For this feeling that I'm feeling
Like the whole world has stopped turning
Like there's no end to the yearning
I've been wanting a solution
To the myriad of questions
In the darkness of my heart
How did we end up wandering away so far?

I want to break the silence
All the things we left unspoken
Let the secret words be spoken
Let the silence now be broken

IMPERCEPTIBLE

You made it sound
more than plausible
You made it sound
inevitable
You have a way
of making
what you say
seem just a moment
away

Rhymes and couplets
Capitulations
So much change
And sometimes static
Involved
in these situations
Topsy turvy
Tumbulations
Role reversals
Without rehearsals
Hearings and perceivings
Are not
Always the same
That sound
Sometimes resounds
And bounds
Around
Again

Surrender and Insurrection

ICARUS: DREAM OF FLIGHT

Did you ever spread your wings inside a daydream
Some flight of fancy imagined and surreal
Could you let the air inspire you
And lift you to the ceiling of the world

Is there any moment more beyond your grasping
An image otherwise than where you are
Beyond your lowly instants, minutes of despondence
Above your seconds, hours of ennui

Take heed of waxing days and feathered innocence
Deny the scoff but measure all the marks of time
Count up the cost of all descending would demand
And the riches gained if you could kiss the sky

ICARUS: ASCENT

Up for it
Up for all life is offering
Grasp at things it's holding back from me
Reach for the beyond
Transcend
And go just go
For all of life's permissions I had waited
Not knowing all was granted
Well before I saw first saw daylight

So give me wings to seek the heavens
Give me flight to soar the winds
Lift my eyes beyond the clouds
to see the sun
Let me not be bound to earth
And not grow weary
And not be moribund

ICARUS DESCENDING: PACT/IMPACT

It was the simplest of agreements
Just what goes up comes down
And for all the desire
To embrace the skies
It was inevitable
to also kiss the ground

Foreknown or no
Some things you're told so clearly
Some things you need to find out
for your own
And if my arms are scarred
from burning wax and fleeing wings
To try and fall into the sun
Is surely better
Than waiting for the worms

The firmament was calling
But now the earth
Must rush to crush my bones

ICARUS: TRANSCEND

Obvious so some things seem
Others no more than a dream
Cannot assume at all that all is known
Or allow consolation what is shown
Some truths don't wait for grasping or to be grasped
Some wait beneath, for miners task
Some wait for marinating allow the juices to seep
Or cure that which otherwise will not keep

So drop the simile and metaphor
To wander through the wild
And enter through the door
To cross the great divide and anger in-betweens
Would gracious arms drop me and catch me up again?

How high can you travel on a dream?
What if reality was more than this?
Would your dreams become wider than the skies allow
Or would the skies applaud in welcome
The impudent intrusion
Find us in collusion
More than kite-like on the storm
Let the forbidding skies
Feel more like home

LAST

The last thing on my mind
Is to not think of you

LOSE HOLD

Ankles tied to sink and stove
The ties that bind
Are common ropes
For joy or sorrow
They remain tomorrow

Hold on
Hold on for joy
Don't lose your artful balance
Don't fall for sorrow
Hold on

Anchors tied this ship to harbour
But sometimes seas
Ignite your ardour
Open seas feel like a need
Will you be free?

Hold on
Hold out for joy
Don't lose your stable
Don't ring it hollow
The lure of free
Can underlap your buoyancy
Hold on

LOVE REMAINS

For all the seasons come and gone
One thing that passing time has not undone
Love remains between us
Love remains between us, oh Lord

For withered flowers and faded schemes
And all the times reality collided with our dreams
Still love remains between us
Love remains between us, oh Lord

I never planned to be elsewhere than here
Because it all revolves around you
And somehow you follow all the way
Anchored in my heart
Your promises and presence guide my path

MAKESHIFT

Slide
The cards into the deck
Play today
Any hands that you have left
Lets make a deal, make it real
Cut the mustard
All or nothing left at all
For us to steal

Pride, so getting good at what we do
So play, the suits are kinda cool
The princes and princesses
All displayed in disarray
Our ambition, our uprising
We could get it there someday
Lets make a deal
So surreal
Cut the candles, blow out the cake
Let's see what smoke we can make
Let's make a deal, let's make a deal

The lights are angling low
But still so far to go
Driving through the night
Is alright if that is what we need to do
Headlights on the highway
Darkness on the byways
The glowing in the distance
City lights so far
I'll stop the car for once
A moment just to breathe and see the stars
Turn off the phone and now
I don't know where we are

MASQUE

Thin papier-mâché
Over my skin
Part of the dance about
To begin
It seems

Sweet tensions in the air
And there
You are

Vintage apparel filled with straw
A pile of logs
A match, a roar
Of flame that time
Of year again

Sparks adrift a colour spray
Gasps of delight
At sights now on display
This night
Alright, ok

A testament to justice
Done, undone and so on
Some guy and friends
Tried to build a fire
And kill a King
But once a year there is this
Another night
Remembering
We remember
But barely grasp
What it might mean

MINING

Incidents and fragments of the
Simple shards of sharpness slicing
Ice away from nicer moments
Warmth abides but not the toastness
All you had was moments of my time
Can you never give them back now
They were mine
They were mine

Telegraph the phoniness
Obscure the crafty draftiness
Abreeze but please unwind the bluster
Muster up the courage
No draft can send the time back
That was mine
That once was mine

Some prizes are worth winning
Some prizes are worth claiming
Some prizes are worth anything it costs
To put your name there on the line
Put your name there on the line
Right next to mine

NAUTICAA (OCEAN BREATHE)

There is nothing
On the horizon
Moving this way
Very quickly
Tack to starboard
All those daydreams
'til they're harboured

Slow the movements
Such the silky, slow and deep
If I listen
If I listen
I can hear the ocean breathe
I can hear the ocean breathe

Who could fathom
Such a deepness
Now surrender
to the depths
So dark and inky
Cold and salty
Full of living
But to see such sea
I lose the full of me

I can hear the ocean breathe
I can hear the ocean breathe

If I listen
If I listen
I can hear the ocean breathe
I can hear the ocean breathe

NOISE FACTOR

Zoning out
All the thunder
In the back
In the back of my mind
Tuning out
The deepness
And the thrumming
Numbing numbingness
Fat blankets
Keep me under duress

Tweak and tweeze
Pound and separate
The real me
From the noisy
Situation
White noise, black noise
Bleed together
Into grey
Just noise

A broken record
Aching tones
Reverberating
Through my bones

White noise, black noise
Bleed together
Into grey
Just noise

NOT SO WORSE

I could fall in love
I could fall in debt
I could fall in deep, deep
Whatever it is

If I'm going to fall from exuberant to terse
Of all the ways to fall, this one's not so worse

I could open the window
I could open the door
I could open the jar ajar aha
But what is it for?

If I'm going to be open, face the universe
Of all the things to open, this one's not so worse

I could shutter the blind
I could shut out the cold
I could shout you a drink or two, I think
I could gamble or fold
I could shoot for the moon
I could shatter the illusion
I could show you the world, if your passport is ready
Pack your bags for inclusion

If I'm going to shout it, put it all into verse
If it's all I could do just to spend it with you
This is not so worse

If I'm going to shout it, put it all into verse
If it's all I could do just to spend it with you
This is not so worse

NOTICE

Did you notice that I saw you
When you walked in through the door
Companion by your side like several thousand times before
The light inside your eyes just a slow simmer yet
Could there be a way to light it?
Could I find a way to strike it up?
Fan aflame the brightness I know is guarded there?

Did I notice what had fallen when you picked it up
I looked so hard but quickly just to see quite who you were
Three words that were not all that small
like a cursory half-promise
Don't expect too much too quickly, yet
We'll soon advance the mystery
Now you've gone begun a history
And I wonder...
Not where you've gone
But who you'll be when you are here once more

OBSCURER

Sometimes the heart finds it all so hard to sing
Sometimes the leaves they come cascading swirling around
Sometimes the bells just chime the telephone never buzzin
- all alone
Sometimes the safest path is far from what you know
I can't find you in the clouds of leaves
Obscuring will they never find the ground?

So what do I say?
So what do I say to let you know?
What do I say?

It's not that I'm trying to be obscure
Simply trying to speak it clear
Without a complication or a mystery
How to build a future and a history
Sometimes just the surface comes to be said
From deeper things inside my mind

So what do I say?
So what do I say to let you know?
What do I say?

And all you are or were I can't find you
All you are or were I can't find you
Where you are

PARACHUTED

Freefall
The winds lick light abrasion as you sail past
Is it affection or derision
Laughter or scorn at the decision
The thoughts that lead to more thoughts
That lead to dreams and then to motion
Action aided and excoriated with insensible emotion
Let it on get it over set it go
Unsettle so
I'm falling
Just falling
To and fro

PARAGLYPH, PARACLETE

I heard you called a GPS of spirit
Go back, go back but would we hear it?
If all we are is turn away and steer it back again
What brings me through the crossing without hesitation
Can flesh transmute into synchronous spirit
Collusion yet not automation

PARANOIA TAKES TWO

A touch too much regard
A bit too little dis of this
Could you look the other way
When I walk into the room
Could you make some plan
To understand
I'm not afraid of you
Paranoia takes two

A scene of mean
Upon my smokin' screen
A hint of less than bliss
Arising from all of this
I didn't need the angst
you showered on it too
Paranoia takes two

So you didn't mean a thing
I'm not upon your mind
Ignored for all the thinking
I've been overdoing all this time
What for is it then
Nobody following
It's no fun
With only one
Paranoia takes two

POINT OUT THE STARS

If you need to sit things out
Remain in darkness for these days
I will not condemn or call you
Where you do not want to go

In blackest night
Let your eyes adjust
to lack of light
And let your breath be taken
By the stars there in the sky

Sit it out inside the darkness
Don't forget to see the stars
And even starlight helps you
See just where you are

PRAISE

If there's any praise
Left here inside my heart
I would want for you to have it
I would want for you to have it
Not that I think you need it or anything
I just want for you to have it
Here you are

So I pull the plug
And let it drain away
It will do me good to empty out
The remains of these days
So battered and shattered
Sometimes I've felt this way
But this morsel of my thankfulness remains

I kept it safe the last remains
The dregs of hope still here
A glimmer still of praise
I want for you to have it
I want for you to have it
Here's my praise

PSYCHOLOGIE: ANALYSIS, PROGNOSIS

Between you and God's memory
Your heart is yet a mystery to me

Gonna light the wick on those Roman Candles
Gonna talk about the truth perhaps
More than you can understand
Hand me some dignity
Wait now for the world to see
Some things won't happen
Won't happen
Won't happen

Got your fingerprints inside my head
Amid my wishing you were where
You were never gonna be
Never gonna be
Maybe

The sirens of the dawn call me
Crashing into your cliffs
Drowning besotted
Lungs full of subterfuge and mystery
Just cough it out
Give me some clear atmosphere
Just simple air and clarity

REDEEM

Some cloakroom in another part of town
Is holding safe a jacket with my heart still trapped
I got a ticket here that says
Any time I want to visit
I can get it back

But who can tell me where that is?
Gotta feeling it's not far from here
Put my feet down
But the ground keeps turning
Turning me around
I'm back where I belonged
Once

everything else under the sun

REQUIRED

Take, give
Take or give or take
What difference does it make?
What difference does the world require?

Use with no regret, but give until it hurts
Eat until you stop, love until you burst
What does love require?
What does love require?

Consume, subsume
Build up and then remove
The edifice remains
Feed your face but feed your brains
What does life require?

Extrude, obtrude, intrude, exclude
Incite, obstruct, constrain, conduct
Incentivise the innocent
Activate what's imminent
What does rhyme require?
What does song require?

Where is sense in innocence?
Obtuse, perhaps, but not nonsense
What is required?
What is required?

Take it easy sunshine
It's not that hard, it's not that hard
Take it easy sunshine
Now it's not that hard

SECONDS

Second words not much to say
We eat our lunch then walk away
Stop talking, start talking
It's been so long 'till back in town
Did not know I would not be around
Stop talking, start talking
Put the blinkers on my eyes so I can clearly see
But sometimes I look inside
not what's in front of me
Seconds ticking tilting over
second best no not today
That isn't you at all
Had to think it over
Does it mean less because it's real
than simply chemical?
Fit my wheels down to the track so far ago
Don't know if I can roam the earth
Unbuckle my round shoes
So much to gain and lose
but lost some anyway
Just one look can make you ask
so many questions
So many questions
Can I afford to look again?
Or not?

SHINE

Day after day in blackest black
Why can you not see through that?
The dark is not like darkest night
If you will shine your light
If you will shine your light

Free-est free or fearest fear
Love will sweep dread out of here
Don't hide away, come out and play
You can shine your light
You can shine your light

Sing all you want to
Shout it out, let it out
Don't let them shut your mouth
Don't let them feed your doubt
Don't let them bind your heart
Unbind your heart and feel the fire
Roast your heart's sweet chestnuts
In this sweet delight
Just shine
Just shine
Just shine your light

SILENCE

If we kept it on the quiet
Stopped down all the inner riot
Turned the flame right down
Right down to simmering

Would our innocence and passion
Still be quite so entertaining
If we held down on the volume
Dimmed the brilliance
Dropped the costumes
Would the world
Stop all the watching
Could we take it out of view
Just me and you

If there's silence left between us
Could my heart beats thrum like violins
Hear the echoes of the intents
Choirs of angels dance on hairpins
It's all there for the listening
In the silence

SIMPLIFY

When there's nothing left
Makes it easy
When you're all bereft
It's so easy

To do within
To do without
To say goodbye to all that
All you don't need

When there is no choice
When it's out of your hands
Cannot know the reasons why
Or understand the falling sky

Pare it to the bone
And simplify, simplify
Rise above it all and fly

(When there's) nothing left to lose
(When you) don't even get to choose
When it's crashing down
The cameramen are out
Got to see tonight's report on the six o'clock news

Cut it to the chase
Pare it to the bone and simplify, simplify
Any choice is a good choice now
When you find your voice

Pare it to the bone
Simplify and simplify
Rise above it all
Say goodbye to all that
And fly

If there was one more thing
To ask before you go
What would that be?
Ask away
So many things
Still need to be said
Life would be much simpler if we did
So one more thing
To ask before you go
Ask away
Perhaps, maybe
There's one more thing for you
To know

SPEAK SOFT

Soft speak soft who knows who will hear
Speak soft speak or who will know I do not know
Listen I will listen if you have something to say
I listen anyway
Can you hear my quiet heart beating
so loud when you come near
Brace your sweet embrace
Your voice like music in my ear
I hope you hear not what I say
So much as what I mean you mean to me
What do you hear?
Soft I speak it soft but mean it for all the world to know
Just let me say your name
And hear your voice and let it grow

SPEECHLESS

Soft, softening crayons in the candlelight
Smudge, smudging wax on paper tableside
Abstractions of denial
Words that won't arrive
Just spiralling, flat technicolour glares
into the night
Waited for the words to come
From either me or you
So it seems, it seems
There is a cat or two
Tying up our language here, it's true
What isn't said we need not undo
Words we never said
Are words we need not undo
But still
I'm feeling numb
When no words come

You said it so much louder
with the look inside your eyes
The empty well, it will not fill
And this is no surprise
So what is there between us
to fill the need inside

STOP GO

Isn't it time
You stopped thinking so hard
Stopped resisting the inevitable
Stopped hoping for less than the impossible
Just stepped outside into the daylight?

Isn't it time
To just own what you own
And have what you have
Exult in the treasure of all that is yours
And has been all along

Could you conceive that it's God's dream too?
Not just your own?
Could you conceive that it's God's dream for you?
And not just your own?

Go for thinking
Go for unresisting, irresistible
Go for hope
Possible, impossible
Surpass the unsurpassable
Step into daylight and breathe the day

THE SUBTLE TIES

I made a little fire
To burn the wreckage that remained
Incensed? No, no anger
And no blame

I think we both did everything
We could against the rain
The driving howling storms
That left us drained

It was all the little things
The subtle ties
That kept us both together for so long
Now I undo that little bow
Loose those strings and let them go
Now I lose you
Now I lose you
Let you go

The torch that once I carried
Couldn't keep us safe inside
The house that we were building
Became a pyre

It was all the little things
The subtle tics
That kept us both antagonistic for so long
Now I undo that little bow
Loose those strings and let them go
Now I lose you
How I lost you
Long ago

TAKES NOTHING

Once in awhile
Forget the worries of the world
Sun is shining through the trees
Sit and feel the gentle breeze

Needs nothing
Asks nothing
Requires nothing
Takes nothing
But to stay and stop
And listen to the wind

And all the things it takes
To get to here
Is nothing wasted
Nothing wasted

Needs for nothing
Asks for nothing
Requires nothing
Takes nothing
But to stay and stop
And listen to the wind

TASTE

Pie in the sky?
I think I wanna taste some of that
exotic culinary delight
But try as I might
I cannot conceive
How I could acquire a bite
When I can't build a ladder
That could reach such a height

TO CHANGE A WORLD

Increments of your substance
Or the substance of your next to nothing
Which is more?
Do you need to be a widow
Mighty widow
To know?
Is giving back to God just like
That drop of rain
Falling, falling
Back into the ocean
From whence it came?
Back, back, we can't deny the gravity
The need always exceeds our reach
But so does the responsibility
And what of the response?
If I can't change the world
Could there still be a change in me?
The smallest crumbs still fed 5k
So who will starve
If I withhold today?

UNFOG

Smokescreen keep the smoke at bay
Open mine eyes to see the day
Don't let to sting and obfuscate
This straining fog must dissipate
One word (or ten) could make things clear
But will these willful obscure words appear?
Sweet muse, keep toes on edge to see
What speech arises from necessity
(Soon, so soon)

VISE

Can I give you a suggestion
A little piece of good advice
Not a squeeze of indigestion
Not a moment of your feist
Wouldn't put you under pressure
Wouldn't tighten up the town
Wouldn't limit all your options
Hold still and do not clown around

Hold still
Hold still
Just hold me tight

When I'm under the hammer
Could you give me good advice
Would you nail the situation
With a flutter of your eyes
An observation, all you needed
To find the key to the steel
Trap inside my mind just made for me
So add it up with abacus
Don't forget the good it does
Let it rain until it rusts
Overpressure 'til it busts
Drug me through the pros and cons
Kick and scream like vicious ones
Just do me good for all the good it does

Hold still, hold still
Hold still
Just hold me tight

THE WIND RISES

Arising breeze
Whispers, hearsay, rumours
Lilting lullabies and lies
Let it blow
Let it blow away

A whirling wind
Circling circumstance
Caught up in the dance
Detritus all aflight
Gravity can't catch this
Can't catch this
Can't capture the breeze

Let it rise
Up on the wind
And blow away
let it blow away

A WORLD TO CHANGE

I want the world to be a better place
Because I am in it
Because I am in it
Reveal the beauty of your face
To woo and to win
A world that looks
The other way

I want the world to be a better place
Because you are in my heart
Because you are in it
And for all the world to realise
The holy place
Is simply where you are

The world can be a better place
Since you opened up my heart
I can show just where you are
I can show just who you are
I can be your feet, your hands and arms
To reach and help the hurt and broken
To say the things that were unspoken
To find the lost, awake the sleeping
To lose the things that aren't worth keeping
To sell the fields, reclaim the treasure
Invest in worth that's beyond measure
Dig for diamonds in the hearts of humankind
Who knows what we'll find?
You know what we'll find

I want the world to be a better place
Because you are known
To be in it

WOUND

Great balls of twine hold us untogether
Unthreaded seamless thoughts of fear and dread
Becoming freedom joyous flying open heart
Unclouding minded, hope and blessdom
Unbounded wounds, not unbroken ever bruising
Let bleed awhile and heal
Let bleed awhile and heal

YOU PAYING?

Reddened earth begins the day to dig and turn
Open up the inner ground remove the soil
and make a castle from the bricks that fall

Wondering what you're thinking right now
Are you paying attention?
Are you paying attention to me?
Such sweet laughter falling from your lips
Is this attention you are paying to me?
Could not begin a dream or write a simple list
Of who you are or what your love could mean
Right now it's simply the sound of your voice
that I am missing
And the sweet pleasure of your company

Saw a simple letter in the mail
Are you paying attention?
Are you paying attention to me?
Got some cooking done inside my memory
You paying? Is this attention all for me?
I'm praying this will never go to ground
Let's create a world that leaves the old one upside down
Let's just laugh and drink the dew
Eat the manna God sends down

Got my spade and shovel, can you believe it?
I'm digging for dear life, I'm digging for diamonds
I'm so tired of being afraid of the good things
I want to reach out with both hands
And take at last all that is real and true
And lovely

YOU WIN

Come on, come on
Enough's enough
There's no need
To play it rough

You win
You win
You win when I win!
You win
You win
You win when I win!

Put away
Your loaded gun
Set your phasers
To cuddle, not to stun

I win
I win
I win when you win!
I win
I win
I win when you win!

We win when we
Win we win when
We win when we win!

Go on, go on
Be big enough to not belittle
There is no harm
In making more
Of all the good in us

YOUR VOICE

Tell it to somebody
Who cares
Maybe me
Say it to someone
With ears for it
Who could that be?

Jack the Whisper says you are the noise
Don't let it drown inside the sea
Tell me
Tell me

Won't block my ears
This time
Won't turn your
Profound poetry
Into a nursery rhyme
If it seems like I'm not listening
Chances are that isn't really me
I'm listening
I'm listening
You'll see

THANKS

Any poet, songwriter, novelist or creative person will tell you not to trust what they provide for you to observe, hear or read.

"It isn't me!" they cry, as if a reader could possibly think more – or less — of them for the power inherent in their creations.

But there is truth in the work, deep truth, mined at great personal cost. It *is* fiction but real life too.

Some of the words in this collection of poetry are me
some of it friends and friends of friends
some of it speculation, pure and simple
and some of it is simply enjoying the gravity, sound and
gravy of simple words placed alongside each other.

I hope you have fun with what you read.

If there is the slightest chance to perceive a twinkle in the eye as you read, please do so. My hope is for joy above all else.

If you are someone I know or have known, or not, I hope you find something of yourself in these pages.

Many thanks for encouragement, critique, inspiration and friendship on the journey; Adam, Andy & Kathy, Angela, Brian, Craig, Graham, Howie and Beth, Jared, Jono and Al, Justin, Kate, Kevin and Jan, Kingsley, Kristel and New Song Fridays, Leo, Matt & Kareen, Mike and Jane, PT, Pieter, Steve, Stu, Vic, Wes and all the you-know-who-you-are people I haven't named, whether for modesty or amnesia.

Many thanks to my family.

ABOUT THE AUTHOR

Martin Fawkes' love of word play began at an early age.

"I remember writing poems in primary school, and the teacher calling my parents in to chat about them, like I'd done something really good, which I never quite believed".

Over time, however, it dawned on him this word play might be worth pursuing. Subsequent years in rock bands meant lots of songwriting, honing his poetry and storytelling skills into musical form.

Spoken word gigs followed, as did chapbooks and self-published collections of poetry and lyrics.

Now, many years later, here we are, a properly published poet. You hold in your hands one of a four part sequence, celebrating a lifetime of writing.

- **Worlds We Leave Behind** (works 2010-2023)
- **Love, Devotion, Surrender and other bright ideas** (works mainly from early 2000's)
- **To Cut a Long Story Short** (early works)
- **Surprise Visitors and other stories:** the Christmas poems